Hey Girl, You've Got This!

Inspirational Stories That Help Girls to Develop Courage, Self Confidence, and Overcome Challenges

Jenn Higgins

ISBN: 978-1-957590-34-9

For questions, email: Support@AwesomeReads.org

Please consider writing a review!

Just visit: AwesomeReads.org/review

FREE BONUS

SCAN TO GET OUR NEXT BOOK FOR FREE!

TABLE OF CONTENTS

INTRODUCTION

Let me start by saying that this book does not know judgment. We keep out what is negative and toxic. Take it as a nice chat with your elder sister, someone who is not too much older than you but can give you some useful advice because she has just lived what you are going through. You are going through a phase full of changes, a time when it is easy to feel lost or like you are losing yourself. It's hard to find the right path. It can be so easy to be externally influenced by others and to lose sight of what is truly important to you. If I'd had someone that cared enough to sit down with me, listen to me, and tell me that my feelings were valid, instead of telling me, "Oh, it's just a phase; you are too dramatic!" I would have probably made different choices. That's why I am here for you!

I am here because, as a woman, I want to tell you that you are doing great! Girl, you got this! At the end of each chapter, you will find a story about an inspiring woman followed by some exercises. As there is not much space in this book for recording your thoughts, it is best to complete the exercises in an accompanying journal. You know what they say; putting your thoughts on paper helps you think more clearly. So, let's start this journey together!

WOMEN'S HISTORY IN THE EYES OF SOCIETY

I know, you have probably thought a million times that being a girl is hard. It can feel like there are a lot of expectations out there about how to look, how to act, and how to sound. Women have made a lot of progress as equals in society but still face unique challenges and pressures. The rise of social media only adds to these pressures; how can we compare ourselves to heavily edited images? Many girls and women also face pressures from their families to behave a certain way, according to old-fashioned notions people might have about "being a lady."

Be honest, how many times have you thought, "If I was a boy, things would be easier"? Many, I know, I used to tell myself the same thing. No crazy skincare routine, not having to care how I look or dress, no period! But don't forget the many amazing things women can do! Throughout history, many societies (though not all!) have told women they are weak. Sadly, sometimes women believe and internalize this messaging and start to see themselves that way, too. One of the first things I want you to understand is that you are *important* and *capable,* and how you see yourself matters far more than how anyone else might see you.

Let me give you a little history class. I promise, it is not going to be boring; I would say it is going to be empowering.

As you may already know, the roles of women have differed and been interpreted in various ways over time and in different societies and cultures. This continues to be true today. The ideas you have about what it means to be a woman are probably very different from the ideas that someone your age has in another part of the world. That's because there is no absolute truth about what or how people should be (well, except for being kind!). Gender roles are fluid and are defined by each culture.

Throughout much of early human history, women acted as the head of the family and were highly respected as the creators of life. Social structures in which women hold the highest power in a family are called matriarchies, and many cultures today are still matriarchal in nature, meaning that women hold the greatest amount of power.

But many Western cultures have developed patriarchal models over time, meaning that men are more often seen as the head of the family or as the more powerful in society. Some research has suggested that this patriarchal model took hold originally in ancient Greece, where over time, women became second-class citizens under the authority of their fathers or husbands.

Neither approach is necessarily right or wrong, and perhaps it would be best to just have simple equality. But it's important to recognize that just because you live in a society that functions in a particular way, that doesn't mean it's the norm worldwide.

We are here to show how women throughout history have managed to stand up for themselves, adapt, and thrive despite their circumstances.

It is impossible to argue with the fact that, over the past century, women in many parts of the world have managed to reach milestones in terms of equality. This doesn't mean that life is always easy for women and girls today. However, many of us benefit from more rights than we've had in the past, as well as a greater ability to network with, learn from, and be inspired by other women around the globe. As time marches forward, we know for certain that most parts of life, including gender roles, will continue to change, maybe in unpredictable ways. But what will remain the same is that your role is to make yourself happy, follow your dreams, and find or create your space in the world. Whether that is leading a company, leading your family, being first in your math class, whatever is important and feels true to you, that is what you can muster your courage to achieve. You get to choose your own goals and values. At times, these may align with what society has traditionally expected of women – cooking a wonderful meal, being an expert at styling your hair – and that's fine! If those achievements are important to you, then pursue them to the best of your ability. The idea is not that you need to aim towards a certain type of life or goal that either aligns with or challenges social expectations; the greatest bold act is to know what is important to *you* and then pour your energy into it.

These strides towards equal rights for women are beneficial, for sure, but they bring their own challenges. While women have taken on greater responsibilities in the world and workplace, they still are the bearers of children and must shoulder the challenges that come with that role. Furthermore, despite the many changes in the modern world, in many places, the man's role remains the same as it has always been. Whereas women have demanded more independence and more involvement beyond family life, the majority of men have not chosen to take on extra family and domestic duties to provide balance for women's expanding roles outside the home. Disappointingly, surveys have shown that in many cultures, women now find themselves in a position where they are still expected to carry the traditionally feminine responsibilities of caregiver while also shouldering the modern responsibility of financial independence and ambitious success. Simply put, women have more freedom, but many of us are still chained by the old and sexist ideas that cleaning a home and making dinner are inherently feminine.

This puts a lot of pressure on females — to meet the demands of a fast-paced, over-achieving and competitive society and the traditional responsibilities passed down from previous generations. It's a lot, and sometimes that pressure can seem overwhelming. That's why it is important to start learning self-care and healthy boundary setting now. To be clear, self-care cannot make up for the inequalities built into society, and it's important for people to continue to advocate for real structural changes that can ensure respect and equity for all. But in the meantime, learning to take care of yourself in a healthy way is important. It is up to you to define what you believe is feminine. It is up to you to choose what is important to you and what skills you wish to master over time. Not social media, not your family, not your crush — you. And you discover that by paying attention to the things that light you up — the things that feel right to you down to your core.

The nineteenth and twentieth centuries comprised significant advancements in women's roles in Western society. During the Industrial Revolution, people – including women – started working outside of the home in factories. While the working conditions for men, women, and children were often deplorable and unsustainable during this era, there is no denying that this entry of women into a workforce outside the home marked a starting point in the widespread drive for women's greater freedom and economic independence.

The arrival of suffragettes, advocating for women's right to vote, and the first waves of modern feminism opened the door to the freedoms we enjoy today. Like many other social movements, the woman's path toward equality can be described as a zig-zag: sometimes there was progress, and other times that progress stalled or receded. The World Wars of the twentieth century actually proved beneficial overall to women's empowerment. Women contributed significantly during both wars, both in the workforce, as nurses or taking over the jobs abandoned by men who left to join the military, and in informal political roles. Mata Hari, a Dutch secret agent, is one great example of these politically active women. Women like Mata Hari and Irena Sendler, who you'll read about below, directly challenge those traditional notions of docile, gentle femininity and can serve as an inspiration to us all.

IRENA SENDLER

Often forgotten by history, Irena Sendler was born in 1910 and worked as a Polish social worker. At the age of 29, she saw the Germans occupy the city of Warsaw. The Germans closed the city's Jewish population into a ghetto, where they lived in terrible conditions. As this was going on in the late 1930s, Sendler began working as a nurse and ultimately became an activist, smuggling survivors out of the ghetto and finding them shelter where they could hide safely. Over four years, this brave woman hid the personal belongings and documents of thousands of Jewish children inside glass containers that she then buried under an apple tree in the garden of her home. But she did not stop there; with the help of others, she produced over 3,000 false papers to help Jewish families from being locked up in the ghetto by the Nazis.

Irena Sendler used her job as a nurse to get in and out of the Warsaw ghetto; that way, she could hide children under ambulance stretchers, in suitcases, or in sacks. She enlisted the help of a four-legged friend, training a dog to bark whenever a German soldier passed by. In 1943, Sendler was arrested, tortured, and sentenced to death, but she managed to escape by bribing the executioner. When the war ended, she went back to work, looking for the families of the children she had managed to save. This woman alone was able to save thousands of innocent lives that would otherwise have been cut short by the Nazis.

EXERCISES

What strategies do you think women used – or could have used – in the past to bring about equality, and what strategies could still be useful today?

_____

_____

_____

_____

_____

How do you think women of the past (for example, in the Middle Ages) understood and felt about their second-class positions in society? Do you think they felt angry or accepted this role simply because they didn't know any other option?

_____

_____

_____

_____

_____

If you were given carte blanche today to achieve a woman's right that is very close to your heart, what would it be? How would you include more people in your movement?

_____

_____

_____

_____

_____

_____

_____

_____

_____

_____

_____

_____

_____

_____

_____

_____

_____

THE IDEA OF THE
"WEAKER SEX"

Although I hope you haven't, you may have heard one or many misnomers about women. Things like women being "weaker" or "more emotional" than men. There are many different terms society has cooked up to classify women as somehow lesser than men throughout history. Thankfully things are changing, but to fully appreciate them, it is a good idea to look at history.

First off, women have been categorized as weaker because, on average, our bodies are physically different from those of men. This is not a rule. There are very tall women and very strong women — just like there are short and very slender men. Everyone is different. However, on average most women have less muscle mass and a shorter stature than the average man. There are biological reasons for these differences that have nothing to do with weakness and everything to do with our roles in reproduction, but at many times in history, these differences in outward appearance have been misinterpreted as signs of weakness.

While many would argue that women's ability to conceive, carry, and bring new babies into the world is a tremendous strength, the duration of pregnancy has sometimes been seen as one of vulnerability – a time when women need extra protection. This may be true in some instances (and a little extra care when they're tired is appreciated by many!), but unfortunately, it has been used as yet another justification for reducing the roles of women in comparison to those of men.

As you can see, the general reasons given to explain women's "weakness" are not actually signs of weakness at all.

We have been discussing physical attributes up to this point, and it's worth taking a moment to speak to emotions as well. In many cultures, men and women have been expected to have and express different types of emotions. For men, anger has often been seen as an acceptable emotion, while for women, anger has been frowned upon. It might be seen as more socially acceptable for a woman to cry and less so for a man. None of this is related to the truths about human emotion. Women get angry, and men need to cry. It's important to recognize the difference between the truth of human feelings and the expectations society has created around those feelings.

Just like men and women are different, societies are different too. Many cultures honor women as sacred for their ability to bring life into the world. In some cultures, they are seen as matriarchs—or the heads of communities—and revered for their wisdom. Even the

Vikings had female warriors known as shield maidens, and their women knew arithmetic and handled important tasks.

However, modern America stems from a history rooted in European colonialism and dating hundreds of years back. In that history, women were considered the property of men. Everything they owned belonged first to a woman's father and then to her husband. She could not own property and often was at the mercy of the men in her life to make any major decisions. This economic structure created many problems for how women were viewed and, worst of all, how they viewed themselves.

There were many women who broke this mold, and there were many degrees of oppression experienced by women all over the world, but I would rather you focus less on what women suffered in the past and more on the strength it took for women to change their circumstances and achieve despite that adversity. Today, you will experience an entirely different set of challenges than I did growing up, thanks to the political and social strides of inspiring, bold, and authentic women. Women who were strong in mind and spirit!

Every day these old-fashioned and derogatory divisions between what is feminine and masculine erode. It is an exciting time to be alive! Let's be honest; you may run into these stereotypes sometimes. The good news is that you can face them with confidence and remember that they have less to do with gender and more to do with personal choices about your values and how you like to spend your time. If you want to participate in body-building competitions, become a real estate tycoon, master stoicism, or compete in sports—you just need hard work and a good attitude to make progress towards these goals!

QUEEN BOUDICCA

Let's take a figure from the United Kingdom this time. England is filled with powerful female figures who fought against prejudice and made history. They have often been forgotten, but today we will try to bring some of them back into the light, hoping to give them due honor. Do you know the story of Queen Boudicca? The Queen of the Iceni tribe lived in eastern England. Her very name speaks for itself; the word *Bouda* means victory. Boudicca led one of the greatest revolts against the Roman invaders.

Although there is not much information about her birth, to date, we have accounts of her heroic exploits in an effort to fight for herself, her family, and her country. She spent most of her life around East London, from a family probably of some political prominence. In 43 A.D., the invasion by Emperor Claudius began. Around this time, Boudicca married the leader of the Iceni tribe. She was skilled with a sword and very athletic, with long red hair. Her husband decided to ally with the Romans rather than fight them, creating an alliance that benefited both sides. The contract worked until the king's death when he left part of his possessions to his family and the remaining half to the Roman empire. Ignoring the wishes of the deceased king, the Romans continued to expand, claiming the entire region populated by the Iceni for themselves. Boudicca tried to protect her own country, but she was captured and tortured.

The Romans tried to bring her down to such an extent that she would be left humiliated and defeated, but this did not stop the queen; it had the opposite effect. Boudicca began to gather supporters to drive the Romans out of what was then Britannia. Refusing to become a slave, she surrounded herself with men and women who formed a full-fledged army of over 120,000 troops from the Iceni and neighboring tribes. While at first, they were successful against the Roman legions, unfortunately, the Roman troops won during the final battle. There were 80,000 casualties, and Boudicca was taken prisoner again, but she already knew what was waiting for her, so she decided to poison herself. Although her revolt failed, Boudicca is a shining symbol of female strength, of how one woman was able to lead thousands of men and women toward a just ideology, protecting her people and her country. Her popularity exploded during the reign of Queen Victoria, making her a symbol and national heroine.

EXERCISES

After reading this story, can you think about someone you would compare to Boudicca? It does not have to be someone famous; it can be anyone, even from your daily life.

_____

_____

_____

_____

_____

If you ever found yourself in Boudicca's situation, what would you do?

_____

_____

_____

_____

_____

_____

Imagine being in a position of leadership where you have thousands of people that look up to you. What would you do? How would you gather support, knowing there may be people hoping you fail?

_____

_____

_____

_____

_____

_____

_____

_____

_____

_____

_____

_____

_____

_____

_____

_____

_____

STANDARDS
AND STRUGGLES

Women throughout history have achieved and overcome and will continue to do so. Yet, in reality, we know we will face challenges along the way. These will come in many different forms, including social pressures, standards, and stereotypes. For many women, these societal pressures start from the time we are young. Believe me; it is a constant struggle for all of us. I want to warn you that I am going to be a little more personal in this chapter because it is close to my heart that you understand how important it is that you be true to yourself.

Over the course of a normal day, women are bombarded with images of unrealistic standards. We find these in magazines, on our favorite TV shows, in movies, and on social media. These may be images of models or influencers who invest enormous amounts of time and money into their physical appearance, and for them, doing so is a job. But for most of us, it is not, and we can't spend all of those resources on how we look – nor do we usually want to! Remember, too, that many of the images you see have been heavily edited or filtered to change the appearances of the women featured. So when you feel like it would be impossible to look like those women, you are right! Even the women themselves don't actually look like that!

You may see trends on social media that seem like they are positive or healthy, and these might be appealing. Sometimes you can learn excellent information online, but other times, what is marketed as healthy might not actually be so. For example, TikTok and Instagram are full of women recommending routines to guarantee "clean," "healthy," or "natural" skin. These words sound great, but the routines often take numerous expensive products to achieve (what's so natural about that?) and are impossible for most people to actually follow. Most "natural" looks are achieved by the use of a lot of cleverly applied makeup, taking actual natural beauty and transforming it into a trendier, unnatural version of itself.

Another example you might run into is content about physical fitness and healthy diets. Taking care of yourself through regular activity and wholesome food is absolutely important, but many of the brands and influencers talking about this online are doing so to make money off of you feeling insecure about your body. That is why it is so important to learn how to take care of yourself by starting with yourself and determining what you need, not because it's a trend or because you're being pushed by social media or influencers.

When you consume media – whether commercials, TikTok videos, magazine articles, or your social media feed – remember that the majority of the content you see is backed by a company seeking to make a profit at the expense of how people feel about and see themselves, and do you know who their target audience is? Us. All of us, men or women, boys or girls. Because the hunt for perfection is not only feminine but also masculine – perfection is not a reality for anyone, no matter how they may look in a picture or on a screen. Reality is the scar on your leg, on your forehead, the lived-in marks, the acne, extra hairs, too thick and too sparse eyebrows, small or big lips, crooked or not-so-crooked teeth, floppy ears, greasy or frizzy hair. This is reality for a human being.

Let me tell you a little story. Since childhood, I have suffered from obesity. Yes, I am being really honest. I liked to eat less healthy things. Growing up and approaching adolescence, unfortunately, I was surrounded by people who constantly made fun of me, called me fat, and told me I would never find a boyfriend because I was too fat. Unfortunately, it's a very delicate situation, and we often don't even realize how or when an unhealthy body image starts. For me, it began with an obsession with models, with those figures that were so skinny, and then the eating disorders started. I'll tell you, honestly, the doctors didn't think I would ever get out of it. I had gotten to the point where I was no longer able to get out of bed.

I didn't see the pain I was causing to my family, including my younger sister, who has always been my biggest supporter. Against the doctors' advice, my family and I went to the Philippines for a couple of weeks of vacation. Believe me; I am not exaggerating when I say that the situation was quite serious. But I knew that was what I needed to heal. Away from television and close to my family, my cousins, playing on the beach— everything that made me happy.

I rediscovered myself. I reconnected with my family, away from the pressures of society. It felt so good to be able to sit at the table with my family and joke around for hours. It was there that I grounded myself and discovered what was truly important to me.

And now, more than a decade later, I am comfortable with myself. I'm not skinny, I'm not fat—I'm just happy. I learned not to label myself anymore. Are there days when I would like to be skinny like a model and have a stunning physique? Of course, there are! I'm not going to lie to you. But then I look in the mirror and see how much this body of mine has given me, how far it takes me every day, and I couldn't love it more than I do now. All this is to help you realize that, yes, it is not a bad thing to listen and observe what is going on around us, what is fashionable or not, but that is not what will make you happy. If at any point you catch yourself feeling sad or bad about your body while online, unplug and find something you love to immerse yourself with. Spending more time with the things that bring you joy — and away from comparisons — will help protect your confidence.

You definitely want to be accepted, but you don't have to let outside fads define how you see yourself or who you are as a person. Believe me, today you might want to be like everyone else. You might be afraid of being singled out as different. But soon enough, what makes you different will be what is most loved and appreciated by everyone. I learned this the hard way.

MATILDA OF CANOSSA

You've probably never heard of her, but one example of a strong, independent woman I want to introduce you to is the Italian Matilda of Canossa. She lived in the early 1000s as a countess and a very powerful feudal lady. In the Middle Ages, male dominance was stronger than ever; aristocratic women were responsible for creating male heirs, while other females worked in the fields. Matilda of Canossa was unique, though. Despite what society expected of her, she became well known for being a great political leader. Her life was not easy, and many times she was forced to escape from dangerous situations. When her father and brother died, they left Matilda, heir to a large amount of money and land. In addition to this, Matilda's mother was connected to the German aristocracy. Matilda's mother knew how dangerous it was for a woman to be an heiress to have so much power, money, and land. This is what forced her to marry a man—to protect her daughter. Unfortunately, her new husband was in trouble with the German crown, and the Emperor of Germany held Matilda and her mother hostage for many years. When they were finally released, they returned to their home in Italy. Over the years, Matilda's mother raised her in the church with a strong spiritual backing, so much so that during Matilda's teenage years, she became an activist supporting the papacy (the offices supporting the pope).

Among the thousands of struggles between the surrounding empires and the papacy, Matilda always chose the side she believed in, even if it meant going against her own blood. Despite the social standing of women during the time, she was respected and honored by men of great power in her lifetime. Matilda sided against the powerful Henry IV several times in favor of the pope, despite his wrath. All the while, under her rule, her territory and the people she cared for reached their greatest splendor. At a time when even a woman's speech was controlled, she came into power over the territories of northern Italy.

EXERCISES

What are some stereotypes you don't like about women?

_____

_____

_____

_____

_____

_____

_____

How do you deal with social standards that don't feel realistic or achievable for you?

_____

_____

_____

_____

_____

_____

_____

Do you feel like the people around you pressure you to follow these trends?

_____

_____

_____

_____

_____

_____

_____

_____

Do you think these trends are actually helping you?

_____

_____

_____

_____

_____

_____

_____

Have you ever stopped for a minute and thought that those girls who seem so cool and trendy are actually struggling as much as you are to keep up with these trends? For a minute, step into their shoes and imagine the pressure they might be under.

_____

_____

_____

_____

_____

_____

_____

Do you ever feel intimidated when you are talking to someone who is considered cool and trendy by everyone else?

_____

_____

_____

_____

_____

_____

_____

Try to write down a list of all the trends you like and that you actually try to follow. Once you feel like you have written all of them down, try to section them and analyze them deeply. Write down your thoughts about each of them. What are the good things about it? How does it make you feel? Encouraged? Hopeful? Motivated? Guilty? Insecure? Be honest; this is just between us.

_____

_____

_____

_____

_____

_____

_____

_____

_____

_____

_____

_____

_____

_____

SELF LOVE: YOU ARE MORE SPECIAL THAN YOU THINK

Ok, I know you have probably heard these a million times from the adults around you: 'Once you are old enough, you will understand' or 'You are too young, you don't understand.' I know you are going to roll your eyes at me, but it's true: you need time to grow and learn. There are so many lessons you still have to learn, so many more wonderful experiences you have to go through and live. Let me tell you a quick story. When I was younger, I thought what 'older' people told me was not true. Call it arrogance, call it adolescence; I thought I knew it all. But sometimes, listening to those who have walked the same path before us can be helpful. I was kind of my own girl, nothing out of the ordinary, but I simply moved slower than my friends. When the other girls were already wearing some make-up, I was still playing with my Barbies. Then, practically overnight, the boys started noticing me, and my classmates started talking to me more and started to find me funny. And, of course, that gave me a boost of courage and confidence. However, I still remember the day I came home from school and decided not to play with my dolls anymore because it suddenly seemed "lame" (even though I was actually dying to comb my Barbie's hair). I gave up everything that actually brought me joy, the things that made me who I was. Now, don't get me wrong, the transition from dolls to other interests is a natural one that most of us make eventually. But was mine sincere? Was it natural? Or was it driven by a desire to be accepted by all my peers? Well, the answer is obvious. I wanted to be accepted; I wanted to be popular.

I remember how I saw popular girls and dreamed of being like them. I found them so beautiful, so confident, while when I looked at myself in the mirror, I saw a chubby girl still reading about Harry Potter. I remember my parents always telling me, "But honey, you are special because of who you are," and "Someday, you will learn to appreciate yourself." I always thought they weren't right because they didn't know how I felt. I thought they didn't understand how sad I was or what it meant to fit in with my peers. Well, let me tell you, I was wrong. The toys have changed, and the make-up styles and popular books are all different, but my parents—and I—encountered the exact same types of situations, pressures, and people when we were young. They actually did know what they were talking about.

At this stage of your life, it's normal to think that being different from others is something negative and that not following trends will leave a lasting impact on your social standing. It's normal, believe me. It's human to always want to be better, and we think that what's best is what everyone else seems to like. But that is not the case. I tell you with all the sincerity in the world that what is best is what makes you feel good about yourself. Don't get me wrong; I also like to look at all those reels on Instagram, thinking, "oh wow, I definitely have to try this dress—this make-up." You know what I usually do? I let two days go by; then I ask myself whether I actually want it because it will be an addition for myself or because I want to be accepted by others. So many times, I've bought something new, and once I got home after wearing it, I looked in the mirror and said, "this is not me." The truth is that if you are uncomfortable wearing something, it is going to look silly no matter what. This has to do with confidence. If you don't believe me, pay attention to all the women in your life who are not following trends. What is it about them that makes you admire them? I bet that when you pay attention, you'll notice the same things I did: it's not about the clothes, the hobbies, or the hairstyle—it's about the confidence of the person.

When you feel self-conscious or insecure about what someone else might be thinking about you, there are a few strategies you can use to feel better. Sometimes I remind myself that what other people are thinking is really none of my business! I don't need to imagine what they're thinking, just like I don't expect other people to try to imagine what's happening in my own head. I can just let it be their business and not worry myself about it. If you find that these concerns still bother you and you're really worried about what a particular person thinks of you, ask yourself, "What do they bring to me?" and "Can I be myself with them?" If you can't think of a good answer to the first question, or the answer to the last question is no, then maybe this person is just not worth it for you. It's not worth worrying about or trying to change yourself for anyone who isn't giving the same amount of care, concern, and good intention to you that you are giving to them.

Even as you're reading this, you might still be thinking about how to dress for school tomorrow, and there is nothing wrong with that. First of all, there is no harm in trying to be and look our best, as long as we stay true to ourselves. Second, it takes time to develop new mindsets and habits. Keep on reminding yourself: you are unique and proud, and that you – specifically you! – are needed in this world. You can start each day by telling yourself this. You can use that sentence I just suggested, or come up with your own message that you find really inspirational, and that celebrates your authenticity, and say it out loud a few times each morning. Over time, confidence will become a habit. You'll find it easier to act according to what makes you happy.

We all have times when we feel down or insecure. There is a voice we may hear inside our heads – this is called our self-talk – and it can be either helpful or hurtful. Use your self-talk to boost yourself up, using a confident, proud statement like we just discussed. If you notice your self-talk is bringing you down (maybe saying things like, "Nobody likes me" or "I never fit in"), then try to put a stop to it. You can just say, "Nope, I'm not doing that to myself right now!" and move on. Only talk to yourself the way you would talk to a close friend or family member: with care, concern, and respect.

Over time, you may even find that the things you feel self-conscious about right now turn into the things you love most about yourself. I'll give you an example.

I moved from the Philippines to a small but beautiful village in the north of Italy. My mom and I were actually the first Asians to live in that town. Although my stepfather was loved by everyone (and I mean everyone), my mom and I always felt looked down upon by the locals. I arrived in Italy speaking Filipino and English; I didn't know Italian. The other kids made fun of me, calling me rude names associated with my Asian heritage. I remember I really went out of my way to assimilate as much as possible into Italian culture. I left behind Filipino culture and traditions because I wanted to be considered Italian. Now, as an adult, I can tell you with absolute certainty that I have never made a greater mistake. When I tell you that maturity and self-love come with age, it is true because that is what happened to me. Over time, I came to understand that speaking Filipino was beautiful, and it is beautiful to be understood by people from different parts of the world. I realized how much I actually love to eat rice with my hands, and that doesn't make me any different from you, from Wonder Woman, or from the vice president. It just makes me human. What made me feel so different as a kid has really helped me in life, especially because I learned so many languages. This sort of trained my brain from a young age, making it easier for me to pick up additional languages, and now I speak six! So embrace who you are. Do you like to read? Don't stop! Do you like to draw? Draw all you want; the world is your canvas. Do you like to sing? Maybe we are looking at a future Beyoncé! What you dislike about yourself today might be what you will love most about yourself tomorrow. You will realize how good it is to be "different" and to follow what feels good in your own skin. At some point, it will feel great to look around and be able to say to yourself, "Wow, I don't look like I'm part of a pack, where they all dress and talk the same because I'm my own pack, I'm my own alpha."

Developing self-love and realizing we are all special and unique in our own way is a long journey that perhaps never ends throughout our lives. Our bodies are our shells that protect a wonderful universe within ourselves. Embrace who you are, and realize that there is no one else like you in this world; even when there are billions of human beings, nobody can ever replace you.

At the same time, remember that those things you are insecure about are probably the same things that the most popular kids in your school are insecure about, too. Some are just better at hiding those feelings. Nobody is perfect, but we are all made perfect by being our most authentic selves. Our imperfections make us unique, and our unique features are what make us memorable. We did not come out of the same mold to all look and appear the same. Each of us has his or her own strengths and weaknesses, our own differences on a physical level but especially on a mental level, and each of us will find our place in this world and contribute differently to history. So, embrace yourself and learn to give yourself some nice and flattering words in the mirror every day.

QUEEN ELIZABETH I

Queen Elizabeth I was born in 1558, in an era where women had no right to free speech and were considered property. In those days, there were kingdoms and empires, and usually, only men ruled. If a king had only a female heir, usually, she was not permitted to rule alone.

Elizabeth had a rather troubled life from her birth; her father, Henry VIII, had divorced his first wife for Anne Boleyn (Elizabeth's mother), with whom he had fallen madly in love. At the time, divorce did not exist and was considered a sin against God and the Catholic Church. So, Henry VIII broke away from the Church and started the Anglican Church in England, of which he was the leader, so he could divorce his first wife. The king was desperate to have a male heir who could take the throne after his death. Unfortunately, Anne Boleyn only succeeded in giving birth to Elizabeth, disappointing her husband to the point of sending her to her death. Once her mother died, Elizabeth was cast aside and raised by several nannies while her father repeatedly changed wives. Once Henry VIII died, Elizabeth's half-brother became king, but only for a short time before he became seriously ill and died as well. The crown then passed to Elizabeth's elder half-sister, Mary Tudor, who was queen for a short time before she, too, fell ill and died. Thus, the kingdom finally passed to Elizabeth.

Under Elizabeth I, England began a period of economic growth. In fact, she sponsored many trips to the "New World," was a lover of literature and the arts, invited artists from all over Europe to her court, and also tried to bring religious peace between Anglicans and Catholics. In short, she was a heroine of her time and a rarity because a woman was typically not accepted on a throne, especially on the throne of the powerful kingdom of England. Her detractors (those who did not support her and did not want her to be queen) worried she was weak and incapable of defending her country. On the contrary, and surely to their surprise, Elizabeth I led successful military campaigns during her reign, defeating the Spanish king, Philip II, who had been trying to invade England for years.

Elizabeth I never married, despite much pressure to do so, and succeeded in uniting Scotland and England after years of war between them. At her death, she left the throne to James I, son of Mary, Queen of Scots, her cousin and rival in power.

Queen Elizabeth I was the opposite of all the female standards of the time. She was strong, independent and unmarried with no children or heirs. Despite the odds mounted against her, England experienced one of its greatest periods of cultural, economic, and political flourishing under her rule.

EXERCISES

Go in front of your mirror, look at yourself, and write down what you like most about yourself right now.

_____

_____

_____

_____

_____

Next, write a list of the attributes you hope you'll have in the future. In other words, if someone were going to describe you 10 or 20 years from now, what words do you hope they will use?

_____

_____

_____

_____

_____

_____

Think about that second list you made. What makes you value and desire those attributes for yourself? Which of those things are already true about you, and which ones will you need to work to develop?

_____

_____

_____

_____

_____

_____

_____

_____

_____

_____

_____

_____

_____

_____

_____

_____

YOUR STRENGTH
AND YOUR POWER

Have you heard the saying, "you are stronger than you believe"? Do you believe it's true? Well, if you don't already, you should start. Let's start by erasing common stereotypes about what types of jobs are best for men and which are best for women. These types of ideas about masculine and feminine jobs are antiquated, and we have – thankfully! – moved past many of them as a society. Today, we see more women than men graduating from college, and women are becoming better represented in every professional field.

You may still hear some gendered stereotypes from your community or even from your family. Some people are used to these old ideas about the things that men "should" do and the things that women "should" do, and it's worth understanding where those old ideas come from so that you can combat them in your own mind. Most of the time, those stereotypes are based on the idea that men are physically stronger than women (so, the thinking goes, they are better equipped to do things like build houses or fight fires), but in reality, these types of jobs do not require more strength than the average healthy woman possesses. Women have been held back just by ideas or beliefs about strength and ability that are not actually true. The human mind is an incredible thing, and it's these *perceived* limitations that can make us feel weaker despite the fact that we are perfectly capable of accomplishing anything we practice and decide to do.

At this stage of your life, where you are changing not only physically but also mentally, it is easy to get sad when something unpleasant happens. Whether it's a math test that you failed, a fight with your best friend, or a romantic relationship that has ended — these situations can all be very upsetting, and it's okay to be sad about them for a time. But remember, *it's a bad day, not a bad life.* You are stronger than you think. You possess strengths and wonderful qualities that others love about you – maybe your sense of humor, your loyalty, or your generosity – and when you are going through a really difficult time, you can practice how to turn those same great qualities *on yourself.* Use humor to change your mood ("Wow, I really blew that test! I did such a great job failing that test – nobody has ever done that better than me!") or be your own most loyal fan and cheerleader (think of what you would say to a friend in this situation ("I still love you and I think you are great no matter what"). Whatever makes you a great friend to others (or a great daughter or sister) is also what can make you a great friend to yourself. Use your inner strengths to help overcome challenges.

These bad times can be painful, but they are necessary in life. If life was consistently perfect, we would fail to distinguish the good from the bad. Every day would just be the same. While maybe that sounds pretty good, it would probably feel tedious and be hard to appreciate or enjoy over time. In reality, the inevitable bad days we all face help to put the good ones into perspective, so we truly appreciate them. The same thing goes for goals and accomplishments—the harder we work for something, the more we value it and appreciate it. The longer it takes, the more effort that goes into it, and the more we will cherish the outcome. For instance, just think back to anything you have achieved. Maybe it's being on the honor roll, earning a new karate belt, learning to ride a bike, or winning your first sports game. All of those things were hard for you at some point. The same thing goes for building relationships with others. You might have to meet a lot of people that are not compatible with you—that are not **your** people—before you meet the ones that make you feel accepted, make you laugh, and inspire you. If it was easy, we might take these special people for granted when we finally find them. As much as no one may like it, life is beautiful because it has highs but also lows.

The best times I have experienced in my life came right after a difficult situation. These moments of overcoming and victory happen whenever we push past an obstacle. Whenever I thought there was no end to darker times, something amazing usually happened to make me reconsider my opinion.

In a decade or so, we will sit back and look at our lives and say, "Wow, I never thought I would make it, and yet I've come so far."

Your mind will always be looking for a solution or a way out because it is programmed to do that. But you have to learn to trust yourself and that the difficult times are all a part of a process. Every tear, every pout, is a lesson that will make you stronger, and one day you will look back and smile, and you might even come to be thankful that a bad thing happened because it made you stronger in the end.

Along these same lines of loving and accepting yourself and acting in a way that is true to you, it's worth talking about how to own and respect your emotions. In happy times, sad times, and all the times in between, you are likely to have some really strong feelings. One of the worst things we can do in difficult times is to ignore or suppress those feelings, denying that we are mad or sad when we really are. Make sure you find ways to get those feelings out. If crying helps you to feel better, do it. If there are people you can talk to and feel safe doing so, great. If you prefer to keep them private, that's okay, too. You can journal about your feelings or just say them to yourself in the mirror. Giving words to our feelings – even something as simple as, "I am really MAD right now!" – is a great way of releasing a bit of the pressure that builds up inside. Think about what you're actually feeling. Are you angry, embarrassed, frustrated, ashamed, worried, sad, disappointed, or something else?

Try to imagine a bottle of water that is filled drop by drop but is never emptied. At some point, the water will start to overflow, and that is the same with your emotions. It is impossible to hold them back for life, just as it is impossible for that water to stay inside the bottle when you keep adding more. Every day will bring new feelings; you have to let some out to make room for the new ones. Releasing your emotions, whether through smiling, laughing, or crying, is a proven way to help. Holding back too often can even lead you to feel sick and especially tired.

You may have been told before not to cry, that it's a sign of weakness or immaturity, but this is usually not true. Expressing sadness (or anger, or frustration) through tears allows us to let out our discomfort. Imagine it as a river passing by and clearing the dirt and debris away with it—just as the water flows away, so will the heavier emotions. Remember that emotions are an essential part of the human experience. Showing our feelings is not weakness; it is strength. It often takes more strength to express emotion than it does to keep it quiet.

If you don't have one already, I recommend that you start writing in a journal. It's a great way to express your emotions on a regular basis without worrying about what to say, how to say it, or trying to filter yourself. Go to a store and pick out a journal that you like, one that makes you want to write in it. You might like one that's lined or one that has blank pages, so you can also sketch or use the space in whatever way feels good for you. You don't have to write every day, though trying to do so is a great habit. Starting out your day with a goal to fill just one page with whatever happens to be going through your mind is a great way to connect with yourself, set intentions for the day, and feel centered within yourself before you start interacting with others. You might not feel like you have anything to say in a journal, and that's okay! Some days, it might feel dull or hard to come up with words, and you won't have much to say. On other days, the words will flow, and you might surprise yourself with how much you write. When you're in an emotionally charged mood, it's hard to be objective, and sometimes it's even hard to find something that can calm you down. Writing down your thoughts, your ideas, and your emotions helps you to detach yourself from the moment, to see things from an outside perspective, so once you have written down the last point of the day, you will realize that you are much calmer, and you might see everything more clearly.

If we learn from a young age to understand our potential, to understand that there is nothing wrong with having interests that are different, that there is no sport or hobby that is more interesting than the other or off limits, then we unlock the right attitude to achieve great things. It will be more difficult for negative thoughts to make their way into our minds because we know that the possibilities in this world are endless and that inside of us, we have the strength to meet life's challenges. So, if, starting from now, you learn to tell yourself that you are strong (and you are, believe me), there will never be a mountain too high for you or a mountaintop that is too scary.

MY MOM

Since these two chapters have been quite personal, I would like to tell you the story of a woman who has always inspired me: my mom. My mom was born in the Philippines, the third daughter of six. She was born in a small town by the sea. My grandfather had a small fishing business, and for a time, everything was fine. They lived in comfort. The Philippines is a country that developed quickly within a few decades, but at the time when my mom was growing up, saving money in the bank was not a common thing like it is today. Money was simply hidden under the mattress.

The Philippines is an island that is often hit by typhoons, and no matter how wealthy a person might be, houses were normally made of hay and wood or palm leaves, so even a small typhoon could wipe out many homes. My mom tells me all the time how her hardship began. One night during the rainy season, they were all gathered in the kitchen with a candle (the light was gone), waiting for a storm to pass and not cause any damage. Unfortunately, the damage came and was terrible. The storm took the roof, and the sea took everything else. They were left with nothing: the house was destroyed, and the boats no longer existed, so it was not even possible to go fishing anymore. My mom's family went from sheltering needy people to being sheltered because they had become the needy ones.

Unfortunately, the older sister (my aunt) became sick with tuberculosis, and the younger one with typhoid. My mom was only 12 years old at the time, and finding food every day was difficult. I want to give you a small picture of my country. Even if you have no money and you are poor, if you live by the sea, in times of absolute hardship, it is almost always possible to try to fish; but unfortunately, fishing for a family of eight every day, and trying to provide at least one meal a day, can sometimes be difficult, especially when it is the rainy season and the sea is raging. The only solution was to send one of the children to work. My mom was the healthiest, so she was sent across the country to work for a distant relative as a cashier. I will always remember when she said, "I left with two pairs of pants and two shirts. Every day when I took a shower, I used the same water to wash my clothes. Even if I was poor, I still wanted to look decent. The typhoon took away my house, but not my pride in being who I was. I earned 20 pesos a week, 18 of which I would send to my family so they could eat and two I would keep for myself. I would see my peers go out, go to the movies, go to restaurants, and I would cry, thinking just how, until recently, I was like them. And now I was barely scraping by, 12 years old with a family to feed. I promised myself that one day my family would no longer go hungry, and I would be able to enjoy life as well."

Whenever I go through a dark time and feel that there is no way out, I always remember this story. With a lot of sacrifices, my mom managed to feed her entire family and allow three of her sisters to finish high school. She had a first partner who unfortunately did not treat her with respect and came to physically hurt her, and at seven months pregnant, she got up, walked out the front door, and started her life from scratch for a second time with a baby soon to come into the world. She told herself, "My parents did not bring me into this world so that I would allow a man to ruin my life." She moved to a foreign country where she was often seen and treated with racism because she came from a poor country, and she was thought to be stupid because she did not understand the language, but she always stood up. Never once did I see her coming back from the store crying because she was looked down on. I always asked her how that never seemed to affect her, and she always told me the same thing: "I am human, I have feelings, of course, it affects me, and it makes me sad. But I know how strong I am; I proved to myself so many times that I am strong. So, I let myself be sad for a moment or two, but I don't let strangers define who or what I am. Plus, those people can think that I am stupid, but would a stupid person have come this far? I would rather let them think what they want and then prove them wrong."

She is the person I look up to whenever I feel weak. So, when you feel like the world is about to come crashing down on you, take a moment or even two, cry all the tears you have to cry, and then lift your head up and tell yourself, "I can do it, I will do it, and once this storm passes the sun will shine even brighter." There is nothing in this world stronger than your own willpower and your will to get back on your feet. Sweep that dust off your shoulder and straighten your crown like the queen you are!

EXERCISES

Do you have any hobbies? If you don't already have one, create one that is only yours — like a safe haven, something that connects you with your inner self. Whenever you feel down, go and do it, whether it's reading, watching tv, jogging, a craft, or anything that will help you feel better. To make it easier for you, write down anything that interests you, makes you feel confident, or relaxes you.

_____

_____

_____

_____

_____

_____

_____

_____

_____

_____

Are you having a bad day or a rough time? What I would like you to do right now is break this moment down into little parts. For example, begin with what you think started it, then write down how you are feeling right now, how you felt before this started, and how you would feel once this is all over. Another important question to answer is: have you ever felt this way before? If so, when and how did you feel two weeks after it was all over? Think of as many situations where you felt similar and then remember that you overcame them — things **did** get better with enough time.

_____

_____

_____

_____

_____

_____

_____

_____

_____

_____

_____

_____

_____

Once you have processed the situation that made you feel bad, take some time to brainstorm what you can do to make it better. This list should be made up of things within your control and should be a mix of things to help fix the problem, as well as things that can help you cope until it is fixed. For example, if you need to apologize for something, do it. If you need to pay for something you broke, make a plan for how you will pay for it. Then, think about how you can soothe yourself and relieve some of those negative feelings right away. What hobbies from the first exercise could you do to distract yourself? What can you do to relax? Are there any small chores or tasks you can complete to help boost your self-esteem and sense of control immediately?

_____

_____

_____

_____

_____

_____

_____

_____

_____

one. You might feel guilty saying "no," because you don't want to disappoint them or because you feel it's your duty.

It's true; sometimes, we can't say "no." If your parent tells you to do a chore before watching a movie, then you should do it. But there are other times when it really is up to you whether to agree to something or not. It is important to learn when and how to say no when it matters. Indulging others' requests every time is not a good practice, especially if those requests, or the work they create for you, aren't in your best interest. Maybe you agree to help a friend with something even though you know you're already tired and don't have enough time to complete your homework. By saying yes to your friend, you've just put yourself in a tough spot where your own needs might not be met. It may be natural and make you feel good to help people out, but if you help others to the point of not having time or energy for yourself, you will burn out and cease being of help altogether.

There is a saying that I love that is good to remember: "Do not keep other people warm by setting yourself on fire." For example, let's say you have homework and chores to do, and you know you will feel stressed out if you don't prep your bedroom on the weekend before the next week starts. Your friends ask you to hang out, your teacher asks you to volunteer for a school event, and your parents ask you to spend time with your grandmother. If you say yes to everybody, you're going to burn yourself out or not have time for your homework or self-care, or goals. This is why it is important to learn how to prioritize what you say yes to based on your values and long-term satisfaction rather than immediate gratification. If you see your grandmother every single weekend, maybe ask if you can see your friends instead. Likewise, if you haven't seen your grandmother in a while or maybe she's ill, and you see your friends at school say, "Hey, can we raincheck for next weekend?" to your friends. Maybe you need to tell your teacher, "I'm sorry, but I already have plans this weekend. Is there someone else that can help?" It might not feel comfortable saying no in the moment, but in the long run, you are prioritizing your own time and well-being without being unkind to anyone else.

Maybe in the scenario above, you plan out your weekend and see that you fit everything in. You can find enough hours to do homework, tidy your room, see friends and your grandmother, and also help out your teacher. Maybe you can do it all, but if you do, how will you feel? Just because you *can* do something (or everything!) doesn't mean you *should*. Sometimes saying yes to too much will leave you feeling drained, emotional, or resentful. For example, maybe your friend asks you to help her with her homework one time. You know she'll have your back if you need it later, so you say yes. However, you feel guilty, like maybe this is cheating a little bit, and on top of that, she starts making it a habit to ask you instead of doing the homework herself. If you continue to say yes, not only will you waste your time doing extra homework (not fun), but you'll feel stressed about getting caught, and eventually, you will feel resentful (and rightfully so) towards your friend for putting you in that position. So, even if you say yes because you want to help a friend, eventually, the habit of saying yes too much can jeopardize the very friendship you are trying to sustain. In addition, in this particular case, you are also setting your friend up for failure when it comes to taking the class quizzes and final exams. If you learn to say no in a diplomatic way, you'll help her build discipline, learn the subject matter, and save your friendship, as well as take care of yourself!

Saying no to another person is not a negative or wrong act in most situations. Obviously, there are times when you'll really need to say yes, like when your parents tell you to do your chores or when a situation seems really urgent, and you feel genuinely happy to help. But it is important to understand and define a line that should never be crossed. Setting boundaries for yourself and for others is important, especially when you have to enter adult life. Those limits represent what others can demand of you and what you can demand of others. When we start setting these boundaries, we might feel selfish or unsure of ourselves because we are practicing how to prioritize ourselves, and occasionally that means denying our help to others. That's why it is SO important to remember that there is absolutely nothing wrong with saying no when you need to. Yes, it's true, people may be upset or disappointed at first if you do not give them what they want immediately, but they will have more respect for you in the long run if they see you take care of yourself.

Always remember, being good-hearted and being a person who helps others is great, and we definitely need more people like that in the world, but it's like most emergency care — you have to take care of yourself before you can take care of others. If you've ever been on a plane, they tell you that in an emergency, you should put your own oxygen mask on first and then help other people. Why? Because you can't save other people if you pass out from oxygen deprivation! If you are on a boat, they tell you to put on your life vest before putting on someone else's. Why? Because you cannot save a drowning man if you are drowning yourself.

It is not selfish or self-centered to value yourself. You might hear this from people in your life, but it is usually from those who want to take advantage of others' kindness and generosity. There are those that will see people who say "yes" to everything as weak. Bullies target these people and manipulate them into doing whatever they want. The people who truly respect you will want to see you happy and succeed. These people will not ask you to do anything that would put your mental well-being, reputation, or goals at risk. You need to realize that you are important, too! Your time is just as important as everyone else's. The people who truly respect you will also return the favor. For example, we help take care of our families and friends because they also help take care of us. Think of it this way; usually, people take care of their guardians in old age because their guardians took care of them when they were young. Of course, family can be tricky, and sometimes setting boundaries with them is the most difficult of all, which is why it is vital to practice saying no to protect yourself.

Learning when to say no and when to give up something you desire to say yes can be difficult at times. It comes down to a combination of self-preservation and values. Some good guidelines might include:

1. Following through with all commitments but keeping commitments to a minimum. For example, I prioritize commitments to family over friends and school or work over community obligations, and I try to limit the amount of "extra" things I commit to each week that are outside of my normal routine. Your priorities might be different. Maybe whatever your church asks of you is more important to you than your grades. Maybe your athletic goals are more important to you than your social life. If that's the case, then you wouldn't want to skip out on too many of your runs to hang out with friends.
2. If it betrays the values you were raised with or makes you feel guilty, or puts you or someone else in danger, say no.

If it makes you feel bad about yourself or insecure or weak, say no.

3. If it risks your long-term goals, health, or mental well-being, say no.

Now, keep in mind it is all about balance. It's okay to occasionally miss one of your exercise sessions or skip a skincare routine for a sleepover, but it's not okay to do it so often that you feel insecure about your body or uncomfortable in your own skin. It's good to give up some of your time for a loved one or carry out a chore you don't like so someone else doesn't have to do it. It's not okay to do these things so often that you feel ungrounded, anxious, or irritable. If you are saying "yes" to helping someone but catch yourself having resentful self-talk or being irritable while doing it, these are good signs that you've overextended yourself or should have said no. Remember, it's normal to make mistakes, and it is all about practice!

When saying no, please remember that you do not have to explain yourself. It is no one's business why you don't want to do that thing for them. Keeping it simple and polite is the best policy. If you over-explain yourself, you may come off as making excuses or being ingenuine. If you reschedule or promise to do something else later instead of right when they ask, make sure to follow through. For example, if you say, "I can't hang out this weekend, but let's plan for another time!" then be sure to actually plan a time and date and follow through as soon as possible. If you have no intentions of following through, just say, "I'm sorry, but I can't hang out" instead.

Maybe it's your assigned chores, schoolwork, and community obligations that feel overwhelming. Maybe one of your guardians asks you to help out with something you really don't want to do, and you feel stressed out even thinking about doing it on top of everything else in your life. Don't panic. Keep it simple and let them know what is going on. Tell them how you are feeling and what you have on your plate already, and then ask if there is a way you can compromise. You'll probably still have to do that chore, but you might be able to do it another time so you can focus on your other, more urgent tasks. Just keep in mind that if you procrastinate, you might risk missing out on something fun with your friends later as the cost of having a more relaxing week instead of getting through your responsibilities. Making these choices is all a part of growing up, though, and they get easier with time.

MADAM C. J. WALKER

Born to a Southern family of slaves, Sarah Breedlove, who came to be known as Madam C. J. Walker, is believed to be the first American woman to become a millionaire through her own efforts, merits, and entrepreneurial spirit. Sarah Breedlove's life was riddled with hardships, starting from a very early age. As a child, she became an orphan and was forced to live with her sister and her sister's abusive husband. By the age of 14, she decided to run away to escape her brother-in-law's mistreatment. By 17, she had her first child, and by 20, she found herself a widow.

To make ends meet and to be able to feed her daughter, she joined her brothers in St. Louis, where they helped her to get a job as a laundress for a wealthy family. Sarah married a second time, but her husband was unfaithful and had a gambling problem.

Like many women of that time, Sara Breedlove's living conditions were not the best. Due to a scalp disorder, she lost most of her hair. This traumatic event inspired her to create hair care products for Black women. In a short span of time, the products that Breedlove developed changed the hair care industry for African American women. There were already several products specifically marketed to African American women at the time, but they were mostly manufactured in factories owned by white people who had little to no knowledge of other hair types. Breedlove's system involved custom-made lotions and an iron comb. The strength of the product was the fact that, as never before, the focus was on African American women and their desire (just like everyone else's) to feel beautiful and confident. Most importantly, the products were created by an African American woman, someone who was intimately familiar with the characteristics of her particular hair type. Breedlove, whose married name had changed to Walker, soon had to hire a full staff to manufacture these products because the demand was too high for her to fill herself. Because of her products' success, Walker was able to open a beauty school and factory where more than three thousand people could work, most of whom were black women. In this way, Madam C. J. Walker became one of the most famous African American women of the era. At a time when racism was prevalent, not too long after the abolition of slavery, she was able to go against the tide and stand out while also promoting the talents of African American women. In addition to her hair care products, Walker is also remembered for her charity work, promotion of African American culture, and anti-racism advocacy. Walker fought much prejudice against African Americans, fought for human civil rights, and during World War I, even took part in protests against President Woodrow Wilson's segregationist laws.

EXERCISES

I would like you to write down some examples of recent situations where you found yourself saying yes to somebody who asked you for a favor, even though you did not really want to say yes. Then write down how that experience affected you positively or negatively. Reflect on how you might handle the same situation the same or differently in the future.

_____

_____

_____

_____

_____

_____

_____

_____

_____

_____

_____

_____

Practice some polite ways to say no. The next time you find yourself in a position where you need to say no to someone, you can do so with confidence. Also, try not to apologize when saying no. In other words, you don't need to say, "I'm so sorry, but I can't." You don't need to apologize for protecting your time and doing what is best for you.

- I would really like to help you, but this time I can't.
- I understand you are in a hard situation, and I wish I could help you, but I am already busy finishing my own tasks.
- This time I will have to pass.
- Thank you, maybe next time.
- Thank you for thinking about me, but I can't.
- I really appreciate your offer, but unfortunately, I can't.

_____

_____

_____

_____

_____

_____

_____

_____

In this next exercise, I want you to write down all the negative feelings that you have whenever you have to say no to somebody (for example, guilt), and then I want you to write a positive feeling that could come from that no. For example, *Sarah asked me to go to the mall with her today, but I already had plans to bake a cake with my sister. I felt bad at first, but then I was happy because I had a lot of fun with my sister, and we actually got to talk a lot, and now I feel very close to her.*

_____

_____

_____

_____

In this exercise, I want you to write down why it might be hard for you to say no. Once you have written down everything, I want you to take a moment and try to put your needs first and tell yourself why you think it's wrong to feel bad saying no to someone. Think about the consequences of saying yes versus the consequences of saying no.

_____

_____

_____

_____

BE YOUR
NUMBER ONE FAN

If there is one thing I am sure of, it is that life is full of surprises, both good and bad. The thing I learned growing up is that difficult situations are the ones that help the most. True, no one likes to do things the hard way, but those are the experiences that usually end up being the greatest teachers of life. Now, I'm not telling you to willingly put yourself in difficult situations just to learn a lesson: that's obvious. The important thing in life is to remember that every step counts.

Have you ever flown in an airplane? When traveling between continents, the height at which the plane flies is always higher than the flights you take inside a country. I've always liked to use that as a reference. I hate when there is turbulence, and inside an airplane, you can feel it a lot when it is raining or windy outside. I remember one year, coming back from a vacation, there was a big storm, and we weren't sure if we were actually going to be able to leave, but for some reason, despite the heavy rain and the wind blowing, the plane got into position on the runway and started taking off into the air. I won't deny it; I was terrified. The first few minutes had been frightening because the plane kept bouncing around in the air, and I could see nothing but gray clouds. My dad was sitting next to me, and he was trying to calm me down and kept telling me, "we're going to pass the clouds soon." I really didn't understand what he was talking about because all I could see in front of me were gray clouds charged with rain. Then by pure chance, I looked out the window and saw that the clouds were clearing, and as we got higher in the air, I could catch a glimpse of a few rays of sunshine making their way through the clouds. Suddenly, the plane stopped jostling so much, and everything became clear. At that point, my dad explained to me that the plane had to get through those clouds in order to fly above them and avoid the storm, kind of like in life. You have to get through the storm before you can enjoy the sun. As terrifying as a situation might be, you have to keep in mind that it is almost always possible to find a solution or wait for the storm to pass. Back to that idea we mentioned before: it's a bad day (or moment), not a bad life! The important thing is to be able to keep a positive mindset, even in the face of the most difficult situations. In times of sadness and difficulty, self-pity can be the easy way to go. It is a quick race to the bottom. Yes, to the bottom, because self-pity only leads to more pain. The question, "but why do the worst things always happen to me?" only leads to more sadness. It is an endless loop of gray clouds overflowing with rain. Even in the darkest moments, you must try to find a small beam of light that can give you hope. That is where the point of this chapter is drawn.

What can give you hope? Anything—a hug, a word of comfort, even just seeing a butterfly resting on a flower—can give you hope. While your world is standing still in that tough moment, any of these things can remind you that the rest of the world is moving and going forward, and sooner or later, yours will have to start turning again, too. It's just up to you which way it will turn. That's why it's important to find healthy points of release and to build a network of people you can rely on for support in those moments.

Emotional support from someone we love is of great importance because it makes us feel understood and loved. It helps us remember that we are not alone; no matter what happens, we will always have a shoulder to cry on.

Although having someone to support you is wonderful, it is not always possible to have someone during every time of need, and so it is important to understand as well that *being your own supporter* is key. Be that good friend to yourself, so you'll always have that confidence and reassurance to return to when you need it. There may even be times when your friends or family are nearby but can't provide the support you need. You won't always be understood by others, even those closest to you.

Especially at your age, as you are transitioning towards adulthood, it might be difficult to find someone who fully understands you — this is normal! Your emotions are multiplying, your thoughts run fast, and every day you learn something new; you may feel like life is going at the speed of light, but at the same time, it is moving as slow as a snail. It is a period made up of emotions that can come like a tornado. It's possible when you talk to some adults about it, you may find yourself frustrated because you don't feel they fully understand you. And sometimes this is true because as much as every human has to go through that stage, your generation has slightly different obstacles to overcome than your grandparents or parents did.

In a life that is one of constant change and revolution, where we seek reassurance from the outside and to be liked by others, we often forget about ourselves and the treasure we actually have within us. Therefore, you should never forget yourself. When you feel lonely or misunderstood even by your closest friends, you will never really be alone. It is important that you learn to listen to yourself, to understand what you want, but above all, to value yourself, your inner strength, and the fact that no one can give you more support than you can give yourself. In a difficult time, reassure and remind yourself that whatever happens, you will be a stronger and better version of yourself! You need to be your biggest fan and cheerleader because you know how you feel better than anyone else, and no matter how much others may comfort you and share words of encouragement with you, the voice coming from within you saying, "hey, I'm here, I believe in you, and you can do it" should ring louder than any other!

FRIDA KAHLO

In this chapter, I want to share with you the inspirational story of the artist Frida Kahlo. You might have heard of her or seen one of her famous self-portraits. Frida Kahlo was born in Mexico City to German parents who had emigrated from Hungary. Her life was full of challenges; when she was only six years old, she fell ill with polio, which caused her right leg and foot to be deformed. This deformity became the source of bullying by children her age, who often made fun of her by calling her "wooden leg," but it was precisely this deformity that set her apart and fueled her creative output in adulthood.

Initially, Frida Kahlo had the goal of becoming a doctor. While studying, Frida became more interested in the struggles against inequality. Unfortunately, polio was only the beginning of Frida's misfortunes. On September 17, 1925, while riding the bus home after school with her then-boyfriend, she was involved in an accident. Frida was trapped in the crash and was severely injured by a handrail, which barely left her alive. The repercussions of this accident included acute peritonitis a year later. She was prescribed to wear a cast for nine long months and to endure complete bed rest for at least two months. In an effort to help her, her mother turned Frida's bed into a canopy bed and put a mirror on top of it so that Frida, although unable to move at all, could at least see herself. Frida's famous self-portraits were born from that time. As the months passed in that bed, Frida became more and more deeply engaged in painting. More than a year after surviving that terrible accident, Frida began to recover and live an almost completely normal life again, despite the pains and the many scars that reminded her every day of that traumatic event.

In 1928, Frida joined a group of artists who pursued a different kind of art from the conventional, far from the rules attached to the popular forms of expression.

In the following years, Frida met her future husband, Diego, who was much older and already had children from previous marriages. Unfortunately, due to the lasting injuries caused by the bus accident, Friday was never able to have children. Her husband was not faithful to her and even had a relationship with Frida's sister. Later in life, our hero of this story found the strength to forgive both of them. Frida decided to focus on her art and how she could help change the world.

Frida Kahlo became a powerful symbol of today's feminism and became an image of body positivity. She continues to be an inspiration to thousands of people. Coldplay's song "Viva la Vida," for example, was inspired by one of her many paintings. Her eyebrows, which are portrayed in her self-portraits, are considered thick and masculine by society's beauty standards. There is a thin wisp of hair over her top lip. Her eyes often reflect her strength, and in the background, she often added strong and beautiful natural images of animals or flowers. Frida Kahlo painted what she saw — regardless of what others would think of her – and because of that, she is an inspiration to women everywhere. Frida knew that being different was okay. Frida Kahlo is a woman who fought; she is a symbol of resilience, who, despite the difficulties that life put in her path, never stopped, never gave up. On the contrary, from these difficulties, she found her strength and made them her own. Her art gave her the strength to keep moving forward. She never hid, despite her illness and injuries or those features that did not fit in with the standards of her times. She teaches, still years after her death, that the most important thing is to love ourselves for who we are.

Frida and her life should be remembered for the message it sends. She was a woman who battled, holding on to life, and taught us to stay true to ourselves without changing ourselves in an effort to be liked by others.

EXERCISES

Write down some of your strengths.

_____

_____

_____

_____

_____

_____

Now write down *why* you are proud of those strengths.

_____

_____

_____

_____

_____

_____

_____

Now, talking about these strengths, what do you think led you to develop them? (For example, I am proud of being an outspoken person because I used to be bullied, and every time I tried to talk about it to some of my friends, they always dismissed it; so one day, I stood up for myself and got the bully to stop.)

_____

_____

_____

_____

_____

_____

_____

Write down the people you are grateful to because they are always there to help you.

_____

_____

_____

_____

_____

_____

_____

If you didn't include yourself in that list, now write down a little thank you note to yourself as well. You are here thanks to yourself, and you have gotten this far thanks to your strength and your courage!

_____

_____

_____

_____

_____

_____

_____

Now take a moment and write out different ways you can soothe and comfort yourself on a bad day. I know this is similar to many of the other exercises, but it is good to keep these at the forefront of your mind to use when things get hard.

_____

_____

_____

_____

_____

_____

OVERCOMING YOUR FEARS

Fear is part of being human. Everything in life has positive and negative sides, and both sides are usually connected to each other. As much as fear is a negative feeling, it is important and necessary for feelings of happiness and well-being to exist and be appreciated. But what is fear? Fear is a feeling that, like happiness, is difficult to explain and is not always rational. For example, many people share a fear of the dentist or of heights. A fear of your friendly family dentist might not be rational, but that doesn't make it any less uncomfortable. Every person who has existed and will exist will experience fear, no matter how brave or courageous they are. Fear is a natural response to a variety of stimuli and is often there to keep us safe. For example, that fear of the dentist might be irrational today, but maybe you have that feeling because somewhere in the back of your mind, you remember a visit to the dentist's office being associated with pain. This isn't how it always works. A lot of people are afraid of spiders without ever having been bitten before. The same thing with heights — it is normal to experience vertigo, anxiety, or even nausea from even short heights if you are afraid of them, even if you've never had a dangerous experience related to being up high. This is perfectly normal.

Something to remember is that without fear, we do not have an opportunity to be courageous or brave. Bravery and courage happen when we face and overcome our fears. Bravery doesn't mean you have no fear. It means persisting *despite* fear. I mean, please don't go antagonizing spiders or testing the limits with intense heights; but remember that every time you feel afraid is an opportunity to express valor in the form of courage and bravery.

Right about now, you might be thinking, "Well, if fear is normal and everyone experiences it, why do they hide it and pretend they don't?" Well, first off, they might be embarrassed. Second, they might be trying to protect themselves. For example, if there is a bully at your school, you probably don't want them to figure out what you are afraid of. Keeping your fears private may not protect you from them, but it might make you feel a little safer, and that is okay. You can accept having fears and be kind to yourself without having to tell anyone about them if you don't want to.

I am here to make sure you understand that it is not wrong at all to be afraid; it is totally and absolutely normal.

Here is the thing with fear. Sometimes it is rational—we have it to protect ourselves. Other times, it is an unnecessary response. The hard part is distinguishing when we should ignore it and when we should listen to those protective instincts. Some of this will come with practice and experience. For example, the more you hike, the more wisdom you will have to distinguish safe heights from unsafe heights or safe snakes on the trail from those that pose a threat. Other than accepting fear as a part of being human, it is also really important to keep it managed, so it doesn't prevent you from enjoying your life.

For example, maybe you are afraid of what people will think of you if you wear your favorite sweater. First off, this kind of insecurity is, again, absolutely normal. But here's the thing— wearing your favorite sweater is not going to hurt you in any way. In fact, wearing it might bring you comfort on a bad day, and it is important to remember that we cannot read minds—other people might find your sweater just as awesome as you do. If you don't want to wear it to school and just want to wear it on your couch after a bad day, that's okay too! If that keeps you feeling safe, that is great! But please, never discard or avoid wearing that favorite sweater out of fear. You like it for a reason, and you deserve to enjoy it.

Another example might be spiders. Maybe spiders freak you out. It's a really common fear. However, you wouldn't skip out on going outside to play with your friends just because that's where spiders live. If you did, you would miss out on so much fun and enjoyment. That's why it's really important to learn to recognize which fears are helpful and which fears are harmful.

When we come across an irrational fear, we don't need to eliminate it. You don't have to go around wearing your favorite sweater to every social setting or searching for spiders to hold. We just have to learn how to be brave and courageous enough to continue our lives — to enjoy our lives — despite the existence of those natural fears. Fear is like bad weather: it might make your day a little harder or a bit uncomfortable, but you still go on with your day anyway. We can't hide at home every time it rains, and nor should we hide at home every time a situation makes us nervous.

Defeating your fears, or learning how to persist and thrive through them, will help you get one step closer to happiness and achieving your dreams. Why do I say this? Well, it's extremely common that people do not make their dreams come true because of fear. Whether it is fear of moving away from home, flying on an airplane, failure or success, getting too close to people, or not saying the right things—these are all common fears that might keep people from achieving their dreams and highest potential.

A courageous person is someone who makes sure that he or she learns to deal with his or her fear and maybe even overcome it. We learn to manage these fears by practicing. It's not going to happen overnight. Some days, you might find yourself backing down from something that is perfectly safe because your fears are too powerful. That is okay. You can try again tomorrow. Take baby steps.

For example, are you afraid of speaking in public? Start by speaking in front of one person, then when you are more comfortable, increase the number of people in front of you. You can also conduct research and look up strategies other people have used to overcome the same fears. You'll be surprised at how many people share the same ones as you. You don't ever have to totally overcome or "cure" your fear. Many famous singers and actors will admit that they still get nervous every time they go on stage. Doing so as a job hasn't cured their fear. They have just learned how to persist despite that fear, and you can do the same.

Remember, too, that common sense is always needed. You need to understand that in situations that could be dangerous for you, saying "no, I don't feel like it," or "I don't feel comfortable" is not a defeat. Having a good sense of judgment in life is important, and you can maintain your dignity and pride while saying no. If you are shy about telling your friends you are scared of heights, and that's why you don't want to use the tire swing that goes over a cliff, you can always play it off by saying what you would rather do, "Nah, I'm good. You guys go ahead—I want to look for mushrooms instead." Maybe you would rather pick wildflowers or just walk in the woods or ride your bike alone for a little bit. If they try to talk you into it or tease you for being nervous, just tell them it doesn't sound fun to you. You don't have to tell them why it doesn't sound fun if you don't want to. That's none of their business. If they try to pressure you, don't get upset—it's normal for people to try to get others to join them, especially if they are also a little scared. If you keep calm and definitive about what you want, they're not going to care later. If they do care, they probably are not the kind of people you want to hang out with.

JOAN OF ARC

I'm going to tell you now about Joan of Arc. Joan of Arc was born in northeastern France to a family of farmers. At the time, of course, schooling and study were not within everyone's reach, and only the very wealthy received an education. Many times, only the sons of these families received an education, while girls were taught how to be good housewives. Joan of Arc, therefore, was illiterate and greatly influenced by her parents' religion. During those years, France was in conflict with England. This is remembered today as the Hundred Years' War. The war actually lasted for 116 years, non-consecutively, and caused many unnecessary deaths and starvation between the two nations.

France found itself at a disadvantage when, in 1420, the rightful king of France, Charles of Valois, was disinherited, and his rival, Henry IV of England, was put on the throne. The English, in fact, occupied much of northern France and therefore claimed their own power over the country. In this situation, many poor French families had to abandon their homes and lands, including Joan of Arc and her family.

During these difficult years, Joan of Arc began to hear voices within herself. The young woman claimed that they were messages from God, who had chosen her to save France from the English and bring back to the throne the true king of France, Charles de Valois. These dreams represented the desire of a great many French commoners, who, with the arrival of the English, had been forced to flee for their lives. At the time, the only "duty" of girls was to marry and procreate once they reached marriageable age. Joan of Arc managed to convince a court that rejecting the marriage her father had arranged for her was fully within her rights. Joan of Arc then reached out to loyalists of Charles of Valois. Initially, she was rejected because of her gender. But she was not deterred, and once the magistrate was convinced, she cut off her hair, which in the Middle Ages was a symbol of femininity. She began to dress as a man and started on a dangerous 11-day journey to the court of Charles of Valois, crossing territories occupied by English enemies. Her plan was to liberate the city of Orléans and restore the rightful ruler to the throne by crowning him in Rheims, the traditional place for the coronation of French monarchs. Achieving this would represent the defeat of the English.

Upon reaching Charles, Joan of Arc requested an army from the king to liberate the country. Obviously, the court was against the idea of letting the army be led by a woman without any military experience, but Charles allowed her to prove by deeds that her mission was indeed sacred and willed by God.

In March 1429, Joan of Arc finally left for Orléans with her army. Thanks to Joan of Arc's powerful influence on the people, she was able to gather a large number of volunteers among the common peasants. Morale was strong, and hope was high. During the battle, Joan of Arc was wounded, but that did not stop her from driving the English out permanently. Thanks to her victory in Orléans, she was able to gain the support of even some prominent members of the clergy. Joan of Arc set off for new conquests until she succeeded in her feat of putting Charles of Valois back on the throne on July 16.

Sadly, Joan of Arc was accused of heresy and witchcraft, and her choice to dress as a man was considered a crime as serious as heresy. Actually, the goal was to eliminate her because she had become too powerful and was loved too much by the people; thus, they considered her dangerous. After a year of imprisonment and torture, she pleaded guilty to the charges against her. At the age of 19, she was burned at the stake as a heretic. Joan of Arc is an example of a strong young woman who decided to go against every custom of the time, from dressing as a man to refusing to marry and even leading an army to free her country from invaders. She has inspired, and still inspires, works of art depicting courage and strength. In 1920, she was even made a saint by Pope Benedict XV.

EXERCISES

Write down some of your fears. Start with the smallest ones that you think will be easier to overcome or persist through. Every day, when you wake up, choose one among them, write a way you can practice overcoming it, and then give it a shot. For example, if you are scared of the dark, maybe you try to spend a little time in your bathroom with the lights off, and then the day after that you try to stay a minute longer than the day before. Soon, you'll probably start to recognize that the bathroom with the lights off is the same as with the lights on.

_____

_____

_____

_____

_____

_____

_____

_____

_____

Think about your worst fear and try to analyze it. Ask yourself lots of questions like how long have you had it? Where does it come from? Did something happen that made you feel this way? Have you always been this way? Is it preventing you from doing things you want to do?

_____

_____

_____

_____

_____

_____

Every day, before you go to sleep, think of your day and what fears you have overcome, and compliment yourself for being so brave!

_____

_____

_____

_____

_____

_____

Whenever you overcome a fear, reward yourself because you did a great job! For example, maybe you talked to your teacher about the hard time you are having with the new subject, and you were scared you were going to embarrass yourself, but you still went, and now you feel better! Then reward yourself with something — a warm bath, a serving of ice cream, some extra time on an art project — it can be anything as long as it makes you happy.

_____

_____

_____

_____

_____

_____

_____

_____

_____

_____

_____

_____

When you are facing a situation that you are afraid of, and you can't find a solution, take a moment, breathe, and do not let it take control over you. Write it down and think about whether in the past you had to face a similar situation and how you managed it, then talk to a trusted adult for advice. Asking for help is a mature thing to do. The answer might be standing right under your nose!

_____

_____

_____

_____

_____

_____

_____

_____

_____

_____

_____

_____

_____

YOUR GOALS, YOUR MOUNTAINS

Giving yourself goals in life is important. Goals and dreams are related to each other, but what is the difference between one and the other? Dreams are desires created by our minds that make us happy. A goal is something more real, or at least potentially real. It is a project that we create, a plan we design in order to turn a particular dream into a reality so that it no longer remains just an idea in our minds. Setting goals in life is an important task, whether they are small or big, short-term or long-term. Think about a car: you know it won't run on the road unless it has fuel. The same idea applies to you and your goals. We all need our goals to keep us going, running smoothly towards the next things we want to do and achieve. Goals help us bring meaning to our days, continually motivate us, and boost our self-esteem when we see the fruits of our labors. Try thinking about athletes. They train every day to increase their physical capabilities because their goal is to win their games.

It is obvious that the bigger the goal, the bigger the obstacles you may encounter on your way to achieving that goal; it is all proportionate. That is why it is important to keep a positive attitude no matter what happens. It's important not to lose your focus and your self-confidence because if that happens, then you cannot be successful in achieving any goal you set for yourself. Defeat comes when, after you have fallen, you do not find the determination to get back up again. No matter how much others may try to influence you, always keep your own idea because if you know in your heart that it will make you happy, no one else in the world can say what is not right for you. Continuous efforts, determination, and perseverance help to keep your focus and increase your motivation.

Whenever you have an obstacle in front of you, you will feel scared, and that is natural, but I assure you that the taste of courage and confidence you will feel once you have reached the top of that mountain will be indescribable and unforgettable.

For example, when you are asked, "What do you want to be when you grow up?" you might be annoyed by the question. It's one that young people are asked often, and it can create a feeling of pressure. You don't need to know the answer to that question yet. But it's still worthwhile to reflect on your ideas. You probably have a number of different visions of your possible future, and identifying those possibilities can push you to figure out more about what your interests are and what makes you happy. Setting goals, then, also means getting to know yourself better. It can mean appreciating yourself and being able to say, "I am good at this, and I want to really develop my skills because I know I can do it."

The crucial stage in chasing your goals so that you can achieve them is not to lose your focus. Achieving what you want, as we have already said, involves a lot of sacrifices. Let me tell you about my experience. I always dreamed of being able to travel around the world once I finished high school. So, during my last two years of school, I started working. I had to work mostly on weekends, and many times I would have preferred to go out with my friends instead of just serving at restaurants to people who were having fun while I was not. With time, unfortunately, some of my friends stopped asking me to go out with them because I could never go when they asked. Many times, I wanted to give up my job and just go out, maybe to the movies. I was afraid that those people I called friends were forgetting about me, and I thought it was the end of the world. By the end of high school, I had managed to save up enough money to be able to travel for a whole year, so I left for Australia, and for almost a year, I traveled and worked and met great people I now call my friends. At the end of that trip, I came home full of experiences and adventures I will carry with me for the rest of my life. I also came home more mature and with clearer ideas about what I wanted to do in my future. You see, if I had allowed myself to be influenced by my peers, I probably would never have been able to go, and I would not have been able to have experiences that changed me as a person. Today those same people who used to make fun of me often tell me, "How lucky you were to be able to travel for a whole year; I wish I could have done that too." But in fact, it was not luck that made that trip possible for me. It was my own perseverance and commitment; my dedication to my goal rewarded me in the end. Trust me, often at the moment, you will feel you want to give up and choose the easier path, but I assure you it is worth it to persevere until you accomplish your goal. Whatever your goal is, you are the one who decides how high the top of the mountain is. And each time you reach that summit, take a moment to enjoy your victory but get right back on track and set a new goal. Be satisfied with your achievement but not content because you are so strong, and you can conquer any win — any battle you set your mind to!

WOMEN OF ACHIEVEMENT

In this section of inspirational stories, we will discuss not one but three women who have struggled and achieved their goals despite their many downfalls.

The first is J.K. Rowling, the famous author of the *Harry Potter* saga who became a worldwide success and one of the richest women in the world. Joanne Kathleen Rowling was born in 1965 in England, and from an early age, she showed that she had a uniquely wide imagination. She wrote fairy tales, which she often read to her family members, who were unaware of her great talent at first. Initially, the writer's dream was to work as a secretary, but soon afterward, she discovered that that job was not meant for her. Rowling decided to move to Portugal, where, for a time, she taught

English, and she also met her husband. Unfortunately, difficulties knocked at her door, and that marriage ended. Her sadness became a powerful creative engine. Many times throughout human history, we have seen that an extreme state of mind can produce ideas and art that become timeless. Rowling herself said many times that taking shelter in her true interest, which is writing, helped her get through sad situations. She often set herself the goal of finishing a novel as a challenge.

After her divorce, the writer decided to move to Scotland, where she began writing *Harry Potter*. Initially, she received only rejections; no one wanted to publish her novel, believing that it was not interesting enough. After many doors closed in her face, finally, her book was noticed by an American publishing house, and once published, it was an almost immediate success.

Another example of courage is Catherine the Great, Empress of Russia. A small game of choice changed her life. Born in May 1729 in Szczecin, she was a minor German princess. According to the customs of the time, she received a good education. She was chosen as the bride of the heir to the Russian throne and proved from the beginning to be an ambitious, clear-minded, and highly cultured person. She devoted herself independently to the study of books about politics to prepare herself for her future role as the empress of Russia. When she was only 15 years old, she was sent to St. Petersburg and was converted to Russian Orthodoxy. She found herself in a country that was unfamiliar to her, far from her loved ones, and with a husband who did not show much sensitivity toward her. Catherine dreamed of a powerful Russian empire, drawing inspiration from the greatest Illuminists of her time. Despite the many difficulties she encountered on her path, dictated mainly by her unstable husband, to this day, Catherine's years of reign are still considered one of the eras in which Russia experienced its greatest prosperity; it is no coincidence that the empress is remembered as "Catherine the Great." It cannot be doubted how this woman's courage and determination managed to bring a wind of prosperity to a country that at the time was overwhelmed by poverty and lacked political stability. Although she was not a Romanov, she showed great affection for the country that adopted her and accepted her as its ruler, a sentiment that was not present in the deposed tsar. She modernized the country and laid the first bricks for a parliamentary monarchy, although she withdrew the idea at the outbreak of the French Revolution for fear that the situation might be repeated in Russia as well. Under her command, Russia expanded, conquering lands in the Baltic and gaining several ports on the Black Sea, an important spot to have at the time in order to trade with the rest of Europe.

How could we fail to mention Amelia Earhart? If you haven't heard of her yet, she is an example of a woman who conquered her fears and followed her dreams. Earhart was born in 1897 in

Kansas. From an early age, she proved to be adventurous and often would set out with her sister. She played sports and especially loved baseball and soccer; she even learned to use a .22-caliber rifle. At only 11 years old, she saw one of the Wright brothers' first airplanes fly at the Iowa State Fair. At the time, she had little interest in flying. After dropping out of school, she became a nurse's aide and cared for injured soldiers during World War I.

She resumed her studies in the field of medicine until she took her first airplane flight. This happened during one of her visits to California. Working hard, she managed to take flying lessons and purchase her own plane, which she named "Canary." She set an altitude record for female pilots. In 1928 she was invited to take part in a historic flight across the Atlantic, and after 21 hours of flight, on June 18, 1928, she landed in Wales, making her the first woman to complete the flight across the ocean. Back in the United States, she was received as a hero.

However, Earhart did not feel satisfied and wanted to make the same flight again, this time alone. And so, on May 20, 1932, she took off from Harbor Grace with the goal of making the same flight completed by Charles Lindbergh only five years earlier, at the end of which she planned to land in Paris, France. The flight was dangerous, and she had to cut the trip short by landing in Northern Ireland instead. She continued to fly in the following years, breaking many records, including being the first woman to fly solo from Hawaii to California.

Earhart, however, was still not satisfied and wanted to be the first woman to fly around the world. On June 1, 1937, together with her navigator, she took off from Florida to cross Africa and Asia to New Guinea. Unfortunately, her great passion was also the reason for her disappearance; in fact, on June 2, the tracks of her flight were lost, and she and her assistant were never found again. There are many theories about the cause of her disappearance, but Amelia Earhart is remembered as a great example of courage and strength of a woman who fought and defeated the prejudices of her time.

EXERCISES

Write down some short-term goals you have for yourself and write next to each how you could achieve them.

_____

_____

_____

_____

_____

_____

Separately, write down some of your dreams and analyze each one of them. See which ones could become real.

_____

_____

_____

_____

_____

_____

Is there a goal you had in the past that you gave up on? If yes, write it down and write why you gave up.

_____

_____

_____

_____

_____

_____

_____

Based on the previous exercise, now sit for a moment, and think. Are any of these goals still in your drawer of dreams? Would they still make you feel happy if you were to achieve them now?

_____

_____

_____

_____

_____

_____

_____

If you have chosen to start again on a goal that you have previously given up on, create a new plan. Divide that goal into small steps to follow every day.

_____

_____

_____

_____

_____

_____

_____

Five years from now, where would you like to see yourself? Write down your goals and your dreams and all the steps you think would be the right ones to take in order to achieve them.

_____

_____

_____

_____

_____

_____

_____

_____

THE DREADED WORD: FAILURE

Failure is a word that can intimidate anyone, even the most daring. It is part of the sphere of fear. Who is not afraid of failure? Very often, when we think of the word failure, we associate it with negativity and a negative outcome. But at the risk of sounding repetitive, failure does not always have to be taken on the negative side. It is difficult to give a clear and structural explanation of the origin of the fear of failure. Have you ever had something you wanted to do but were so afraid of failure that you decided to put it aside? Failure does not just mean not getting the desired result from a project or a class assignment. The fear of failure also comes from the fear of disappointing someone else. As impossible as it may seem, it is possible to master the fear of failure, just as it is possible to succeed in seeing the positive side of failure. When you are young, making mistakes is part of everyday life. Why? Because we are like sponges, we are not born knowing everything. We learn as we go, and the best way to learn is to fail. We are constantly influenced by what is around us, and, as we have seen in past chapters, attitude and common sense are what matter. The fear of failing to achieve one's goals can immobilize us; it can cause us to feel defeated and give up, sometimes before we even get started. Clearly, when we allow fear to stop our plans, we risk losing numerous opportunities along the way.

But let's try to take a closer look together at this big monster that actually is not so big.

Each of us has a specific idea of what is meant by failure: what for one person represents a big experience of failure for another may represent an opportunity for growth. Fear of failure can be related to many causes, such as having critical or unsupportive parents, not having a good support system, having people that always point out what you've done wrong instead of what you accomplished along the way, and not having enough faith in our own strength and abilities.

Another cause could be having experienced an event that was very difficult and which created its own fear. For example, making a really bad or embarrassing presentation in front of an audience could lead a person to experience fear of failure and therefore avoid similar situations in the future.

It is almost impossible to go through life without experiencing some form of failure. As with any experience, the amazing thing about failure is that we decide what value and meaning we want to attach to it. We can choose to see failure as "the end of the world" or as the test of our inability, or we can look at it as an opportunity for learning and growth.

I think the right approach to take when faced with an act or a challenge is not to give too much importance to the outcome or create a negative meaning for our mistakes. We should throw ourselves into new activities as we threw ourselves into learning to walk as children: without the fear of falling or being judged incapable during our falls. At best, we got back up and gave it another try.

Standing motionless, paralyzed by the fear of not succeeding, causes you to miss great opportunities and not live the life you deserve. People who are overly afraid of failure might be afraid to try new things in general and be really stuck in their limited comfort zone. They may self-sabotage by procrastinating or not setting goals so that they don't ever have to do anything that pushes them outside of that comfort zone.

Fear of failure can also lead to low self-esteem or low self-confidence, which might show up in negative self-talk like, "I will never be able to get that promotion," or "I am not good enough to join that team."

Fear of failure can contribute to perfectionism, which is the tendency to try only those things you know you will be able to complete perfectly. This might not sound so bad, but it's not a great way to live. A perfectionist might be very self-critical and limit new experiences.

Believe it or not, every feeling we experience also has an effect on our bodies. Have you ever been so afraid that you couldn't eat? Or even the opposite, have you ever found yourself eating some extra candies because you are stressed? This happens to me very often! And when I realize it, I sit and wonder why; what is my body trying to tell me? The mind is such an amazing tool; it often tries to communicate with us through our bodies. And so is the case with the fear of failure. When you realize that something in your body or in your habits is changing, try sitting down for a moment. Learn to listen to yourself and understand what you need.

So when you inevitably do face failures along the path to your goals, that's okay. Your first (or second, or third) plans or attempts might not work out. You can take a little bit of time to feel disappointed about that and then pick yourself up and make a new plan.

So instead of saying, "I'm a failure, I couldn't do it," you have to say to yourself, "hey, I had no idea that actually I was supposed to do that. At least now I know something more than I did before." There are so many wonderful things about this! You will come out even stronger, have a broader perspective, and you can help others not make the same mistake you made.

Another piece of advice I can give you is to visualize your ultimate goal but create small goals along the way to lead you toward that big one. Always remember that the pyramids were not built in a few days; each block was worked on and studied. Bigger things take time and patience.

The final piece of advice: face everything with pride in yourself. Believe me, even if you don't feel like it, look in the mirror and smile at yourself. When you felt that strong fire inside you, that desire to achieve your dream, you got up and rolled up your sleeves, so be proud of yourself because I am proud of you! That strength you feel inside your chest, listen to it, cherish it, and nurture it because you are a woman, and you are an amazing being!

I'll share another example with you of a dream that came true. My sister and I always loved the idea of being able to open a small bed and breakfast in our family home. We have fantastic memories in that house, and the idea that we could allow other people to have those feelings have always fascinated us. A good chunk of our childhood took place between the green woods behind our house and the laughter on the balcony during summer evenings. And so, one day, we decided to roll up our sleeves and give it a try; after all, we had nothing to lose. I won't deny it; the fear was tremendous! Not only the fear of failure, but we would have to spend some money, which wasn't easy for us, and it would take an enormous amount of time to get the house in shape. But our dream was so big and strong, and so we set to work. It took us six years to do everything. Where others have managed to open a bed & breakfast in a few months, we had to fail quite a few times before we could reach our goal. The first year we officially opened, we were forced to close again after a week because the authorities realized that we had actually turned in the wrong documents. Think of the frustration and disappointment of that moment. More than once, I thought about giving up. After the third attempt, I was exhausted, and I began to doubt this great dream. Do you know what gave me the energy to continue? The image of another family with children laughing and creating memories to carry with them for the rest of their lives on that small terrace, where in the summer it is filled with green ivy climbing the walls, the small vineyard serving as a roof, and colorful flowers poking from every corner. And so, after a full six years, we have finally succeeded in our dream, and every year, even if only for a few months, we have the opportunity to meet fantastic people who often write and thank us because they had a great vacation and they created memories that will remain permanent in their minds.

So, if you have a dream you want to achieve, do it! Create your own path, and break down all those barriers; trust me, your heart will go crazy with joy once you realize your dreams!

MARIE CURIE

In this inspirational story, we will talk about a woman who made a great contribution to humanity. Her studies and interests caused her death, but her perseverance saves thousands of people every day. Her name is Marie Curie. Curie was born in Warsaw, Poland, as Maria Skłodowska. She was a very intelligent child, and her interest in studying was clear through her grades in school. Unfortunately, in her country at that time, women could not go to high school, so Curie and her sister began studying at a secret school called "The Floating Academy." The two sisters, tired of hiding, discovered one day that there was a university in Paris that also accepted girls. Thus, they decided to move to France.

Marie Curie was very fascinated by physics, metals, and magnets, and she discovered that some elements gave off powerful rays and glowed in the dark. In order to analyze these minerals, she tried to reduce them into even coarser materials by burning and melting them and finally filtering them so that she could study them. After all these years, Marie Curie's instruments and notebooks are not accessible to everyone because they are radioactive! That's right, the materials she studied and was fascinated with caused radioactivity. In order to look at her notebooks, one has to wear protective suits and gloves. Curie, as we have already mentioned, died as a result of her studies because contact with these materials caused her to get aplastic anemia, a disease that is contracted from long exposures to radiation. Marie Curie is buried at the Pantheon in Paris, and her coffin is wrapped in a lead shirt to prevent radioactivity from escaping.

Thanks to Marie Curie, today we know the elements called "radium" and "polonium." Thanks to these very discoveries, Marie Curie was the first woman in history to receive a Nobel Prize. Sometime later, her husband, who was teaching at the Sorbonne in Paris, was the victim of a terrible accident. Curie immediately took her husband's place in the classroom to make sure that his students did not miss a single day of study. Her husband taught physics, and she continued her own research in this field, ultimately winning a second Nobel Prize. Marie Curie's discoveries were immediately used in medicine and became very important, especially in times of war. Later in life, Curie founded a school in Paris to help girls study and follow their dreams. Marie Curie is a symbol of redemption for women all over the world. She became a world-renowned scientist, university teacher, and winner of two Nobel Prizes.

EXERCISES

Have you ever given up a dream because you were scared to fail? Have you ever tried to do something you really wanted to do but then gave up after you failed? Write about your experience.

_____

_____

_____

_____

_____

_____

Do you regret giving up a dream? Would you take it up again?

_____

_____

_____

_____

_____

_____

_____

CONCLUSION

What should we take from this book?

It is obvious that my words are not law; they are from my experiences and my desire to be able to give you guidance. After reading this book, I hope you have learned or at least started to recognize your importance. Life is not a fairy tale; I can tell you that for sure; however, it is great for what it is. Every day is an adventure. There will be days of defeat and victory, but you should never lose your strength and courage. Remember that in this world, there are billions of people walking around every day, and fads are not the law. Always remember your importance and the fact that you are not here to be accepted by following rules imposed by others. You are here to live your diversity and authenticity without obligation to follow any standards. Don't get carried away by what others say.

There are no instructions to beauty, but the first step is goodness of heart toward ourselves and others. This requires sensitivity to accepting what is different from us and also respecting the tastes and opinions of others, even if we do not like or agree with them. We have seen that throughout history, many women have been overshadowed, and we are here today to make our voices heard.

We take our example from the women before us who stood up and said, "No, I'm not going to stand for this. No, I want to live my life; I don't want to just exist under the rules imposed by men who are afraid of female strength." So, like many other brave women, follow your goals, believe in your dreams, but above all, have confidence in your abilities and never be afraid to make mistakes; it is only by making mistakes that you learn. You made mistakes a thousand times before you learned how to write correctly, and this applies to all aspects of life. So whenever you fall, always get back up and sweep the dust off your shoulder with pride. Don't be afraid to challenge yourself, to challenge the world. Never doubt your ability, your strength, but most of all, your intelligence. Never let grades in school define how smart you are because everyone has different abilities and can shine where they are most skilled. And occasionally, stop and congratulate yourself because being strong is hard work, but no one else can do it better than you! A woman's strength is incredible and puts to rest any thoughts and ideas of the "weaker sex."

On this journey, remember your brave sisters but also your brave brothers (hey, we are here to create a better future where everyone is equal and equally important).

We can learn from the past to create a better future. And last but not least, always keep in mind that accepting help from others and offering our help to others is not a sign of weakness but a sign of great awareness that to grow, it is important to have an open mind.

Thank you for taking this journey with me; I hope that at the end of it all, you feel stronger and that you have become aware of your strength by recognizing it in all the things you do, even the most insignificant! And I hope you've learned to love yourself, to cherish all those details that make you who you are. Own them and parade them as the most shining jewel that belongs to a queen like you! Girl, you definitely got this, and I am so proud of you!